Sam and Kit Can Nap

Written by
Stephen Rickard

Illustrated by
Emma Proctor

Sam and Kit can nap in a cot.

Sam and Kit can nap in a pot.

Sam and Kit can nap on a mat.

Sam and Kit can nap on a cat.

Sam and Kit can nap in a pan.

Sam and Kit can nap on Nan.

Sam and Kit can not nap on a dog!